THE FUNNIEST LEICESTER QUOTES... EVER!

Also available

THE FUNNIEST LEICESTER QUOTES... EVER!

by Gordon Law

Printed in Europe and the USA
ISBN: 9798693012684
Imprint: Independently published

Photos courtesy of: Influential Photography/Shutterstock.com; Michael Hulf.

Contents

Introduction

Claudio Ranieri's "Dilly ding, dilly dong" catchphrase became one of the memorable parts of his time as Leicester City boss.

Ranieri revealed the quirky saying was his way of motivating the players when he thought they were sleeping and it was one of his many sound bites that had reporters in stitches.

His tongue-in-cheek comments would light up the press room, whether it was about buying pizzas for the squad, likening them to Forrest Gump or having a Kasabian love-in as he steered Leicester to title-winning glory.

The affable Italian is not the only colourful character to have made his mark at the club with amusing anecdotes, bonkers boasts or witty one-liners.

Ian Holloway is a comedy genius and loves to come out with a hilarious analogy, angry rant at the referee or a sarcastic quip.

Fellow Foxes managers Martin O'Neill, Dave Bassett and Micky Adams also enjoyed reeling off unforgettable remarks during their time in the hot seat.

Leicester players have also kept us chuckling, whether it's Jamie Vardy's bizarre pre-match rituals, Robert Huth's comical tweets or Frank Worthington's off-the-pitch antics.

Many of their foot-in-mouth moments can be found in this unique collection of funny Leicester quotes and I hope you laugh as much reading this book as I did in compiling it.

Gordon Law

THE FUNNIEST LEICESTER QUOTES... EVER!

MANAGING JUST FINE

"No one gave us a chance of surviving in the Premiership except for some paper in Bulgaria that said we'd stay up. I'm going to write and thank them."

Martin O'Neill

"I told my side that their defence is crap but the other six are f*cking brilliant."

Dave Bassett reveals his team talk before facing Manchester United

"If my aunt had balls, she'd be my uncle."

Martin Allen on whether he would have gone to Leicester if MK Dons had reached the play-off final

"The last time I met him, I won 2-1 in the Champions League quarter-final with Chelsea. He forgot, but I remember. I will tell him Sunday, 'You forgot, I won, you lose'... I remember when I want to remember."

Claudio Ranieri jokes about his record against Arsene Wenger

"I am waiting for the whole stadium to sing, 'Dilly ding, dilly dong!'."

Claudio Ranieri

"Be smart – you are Foxes!"

Claudio Ranieri's message to the players before each game

"I asked if I could speak to Mr Steve Bruce. The man who picked up the phone said he was training and I replied in my Scottish accent that it was Sir Alex Ferguson on the phone. Mr Bruce came to the phone and said, 'Good morning Alex' and I replied, 'Good morning Steve, it's Martin Allen'. He laughed and laughed and laughed. He called me a few names, I got the answer out of him that I wanted and we got the [DJ Campbell] deal completed."

Martin Allen

"I pay for pizza, you pay for the sausage. I am the sausage man."

Claudio Ranieri after a Leicester butcher had created a sausage in his honour

"Half-jokingly, I asked [David Beckham] if he wanted to move back to England and come play for us. David said that it sounded interesting... But Victoria looked at me as if I was mad. 'Sven', she said. 'Could you see me in Leicester?' David laughed and said, 'When we lived in Madrid, it wasn't posh enough for my wife."

Sven-Goran Eriksson

"We've got to go there and tweak the nose of fear and stick an ice cube down the vest of terror. That's not an Ian Holloway quote, by the way. It's Blackadder."

Ian Holloway before a big game against Stoke

"We are in the Champions League, dilly ding, dilly dong – come on. We are in the Champions League, it is fantastic, terrific. Well done to everybody."

Claudio Ranieri

"You'd need to start bribing the opposition or paying their wage bill."

Dave Bassett when asked how Leicester could avoid relegation

"If we do go down it will be just like the day I found out Father Christmas was really my dad."

Micky Adams

"There is a saying in Italy that you do not sell the bear's skin until you have shot it."

Claudio Ranieri

"It's a football club, not a prison. People shouldn't see me coming and think, 'Oh here's the b*stard'."

Ian Holloway doesn't want to be feared at Leicester

"I'd like to say, 'Yes we can!' But I am not Barack Obama!"

Claudio Ranieri on whether Leicester can shock the world and win the league

"I told them, if you keep a clean sheet, I'll buy pizza for everybody. I think they're waiting for me to offer a hot dog too."

Claudio Ranieri's prize to his players before they finally kept their first clean sheet of the season after a 1-0 win over Palace

"We'll be a force to be reckoned with. When that will be, I'm not 100 per cent sure."

Craig Levein

"I wouldn't quote Kipling to the lads. They'd probably think I was talking about cakes."

Rob Kelly

"Watching Chelsea on Monday I was at first on the armchair, but after [the Hazard goal] on the ceiling!"

Claudio Ranieri after Eden Hazard levelled against Spurs to clinch Leicester's title

"There's not as much quality in the team as I thought, so it has proven difficult. I'm not saying the team is useless..."

Dave Bassett... or are you?

"Luck is the salt, the fans are the tomato – with no tomato there is no pizza."

Claudio Ranieri

"Why can't we continue to run, run, run? We are like Forrest Gump. Leicester is Forrest Gump. I give you the headline there."

Claudio Ranieri ahead of an encounter with Liverpool

"I will kill them with my bare hands, I will throttle them!"

Claudio Ranieri warns his players before a crunch clash with Everton

"Sometimes we sit at the dinner table and I am frightened at how much they eat. I've never seen players so hungry!"

Claudio Ranieri on his famished squad

"I told my players, 'When you go on the pitch and you hear the song from Kasabian, that means they want warriors'. I want to see them as warriors for the fans. Kasabian are a fantastic rock band from Leicester and I think the guitar man, Serge, is Italian."

Claudio Ranieri

"If someone in the crowd spits at you, you've just got to swallow it."

Gordon Milne's advice to Gary Lineker

"Seeing the police be happy, it makes me happy!"

Claudio Ranieri at Leicester's title parade

"Tomorrow, training session. Bad lads!"

Claudio Ranieri on what's in store for the players after Christian Fuchs sprayed him with champagne on the season's final day

Dave Bassett: "I can't learn a foreign language because of my dyslexia. I read a lot of things that don't make any sense. I often get my d's and b's mixed up."

Journalist: "It makes you wonder whether you have bought the wrong player by mistake."

Dave Bassett: "Yeah, well, I've claimed that a couple of times. But the chairman wasn't impressed."

"I tell them, 'Dilly ding, dilly dong!' From the beginning when something was wrong, I said, 'Hey, dilly ding, dilly dong! Wake up!' And during all the training sessions sometimes I say, 'Dilly ding, dilly dong'. Then for Christmas day, I brought all the players and staff, everybody, a little bell just to joke. It was a funny thing."

Claudio Ranieri gives some insight into one of his motivational techniques

"I feel like that fellow off the Ready Brek advert who's got that red glow around him all day."

Martin Allen ahead of the new season

"It looks as if I am trying to stab Dave Bassett in the back but I'm not holding a gun to anybody's head."

Micky Adams

"I don't know English that well. I can hear them saying, 'Ranieri' and something else. I hope they're praising me!"

Claudio Ranieri on the fan chants

"I don't believe the bookmakers. At the beginning of the season the bookmakers said, 'Sack Ranieri'. I hope one time they are right!"

Claudio Ranieri on the news Leicester had been made favourites for the title

"It will be a very good atmosphere with the music. I hope we are ready, not just to listen to the music but to do some music."

Claudio Ranieri is looking forward to the Champions League

"My players are earning bloody good money and they've got to take responsibility for earning that money. It's lucky we're not brain surgeons or airline pilots or we'd have a few murders on our hands."

Dave Bassett

Leicester fan: "It's pantomime season out there!"
Nigel Pearson: "Oh no it isn't!"

"My team is like an orchestra. To play the symphony correctly I need some of the boom boom boom, but I also need some tweet and sometimes the tweet and boom go well together. Sometimes all you can hear is the boom, sometimes only the tweet. That is not good music."

Claudio Ranieri

"In terms of a 15-round boxing match, we're not getting past round one. Teams will pinch your dinner from under your noses. If you don't heed the warnings, you get nailed to the cross."

Gordon Milne

"It's fantastic when you see before the match, an old lady with a Leicester shirt outside the stadium. I say, 'Unbelievable. They come from Leicester to support us'. This is my emotion."

Claudio Ranieri on the Foxes going 10 points clear at the top in April 2016

"Sometimes when you aim for the stars, you hit the moon."

Ian Holloway on his forward line

"Yes, big revenge, I want to kill him... He's a nice man. It's just football."

Claudio Ranieri on facing Watford's Quique Sanchez Flores, who replaced him at Valencia

"The day my players relax I get crazy. They know that. I think I am a nice man but also I am demanding."

Claudio Ranieri

"I don't care whether you are Alan Shearer or the Pope; you don't do things like that."

Martin O'Neill slams David Beckham for his England red card against Argentina

"It is important to finish the story like an American movie. Always in the end it is OK. There is a happy ending."

Claudio Ranieri wants the fairytale ending to the season

"No pizza tonight, our chairman has invited us to dinner."

Claudio Ranieri

"Wouldn't it be great to go to a club that's boring, where nothing happens?"

Micky Adams on quitting his post after the club went into administration and then got promoted and relegated

"Now we need a bigger incentive. I might have to buy lunch or dinner next season... maybe lobster. Only one."

After the pizza, Claudio Ranieri ups the ante for 2016/17

"If I could have imagined the perfect ending to this story for Leicester, this is precisely the way I would have imagined it, with Bocelli singing 'Vincero' in the middle of the stadium."

Claudio Ranieri on the amazing finale

"I have spent nothing – and if you look at my squad it is probably worth nothing."

Micky Adams

"It's important not to look down or behind you. Like a climber, you need to look up. If you look down, you go, 'Oh! My God, look where we are!"

Claudio Ranieri

"It's all very well having a great pianist playing, but it's no good if you haven't got anyone to get the piano on the stage in the first place. Otherwise the pianist would be standing there with no bloody piano to play."

Ian Holloway on his limited squad

"I want to be the most crazy man and team in the Premier League."

Claudio Ranieri on Leicester remaining top in mid January 2016

"Three people and five cabbages."

Dave Bassett describes the average Foxes home crowd

"It's easier for ET to come to Piccadilly Circus. It is more difficult than last season. It is normal that we can't win the league. For this reason, I say the bookmakers must do 6,000-1. I am very curious, all the world is curious, what will happen with Leicester. I am very curious to see where we finish."

Claudio Ranieri plays down Leicester's chances of another title win

"It should be a good match because they're a good football team as well and we're a good football team. It should be a very good match."

Peter Taylor is feeling good

"Now there are a lot of sharks, and I am on the windsurfer. I accept this. This is our life. Last season was a fairytale, this season is not a fairytale. But it is OK. Now it is important to be positive without bad, bad words."

Claudio Ranieri on Leicester's change in fortunes

"I wouldn't know a Monet if it hit me in the mouth. I might be tempted to put up a Page 3 picture, but I don't think I'd be allowed. I used to get those Pirelli calendars but somehow I came off the mailing list."

Dave Bassett on his office at the training ground

THE FUNNIEST LEICESTER QUOTES... EVER!

MEDIA CIRCUS

Jeff Stelling: "It's an old cliche but is this a must-win game for you?"

Micky Adams: "Shreevesy, I can't believe you're trying to say we can't go to Man U and Arsenal and win."

Stelling: "Who's this Shreevesy? It's Stelling, not Shreeves. He's the fat one, haha... Look, Tony Adams, er Micky Adams, thanks very much indeed."

Q: "Has Vardy signed a new contract?"

Claudio Ranieri: "I don't know. I'm not the manager, I'm just head coach. I'm sorry, haha. Pinocchio!"

"Would be worse turning up holding a Sun newspaper I guess."

James Maddison responds to the Sun's story: 'James Maddison arrives for Spurs clash wearing horrific £6,500 backpack'

"Ay, you are sleeping, come on!"

Claudio Ranieri wakes up a reporter before dinging his bell

"I am dilly ding, dilly dong. I am a bell, haha. Don't write, 'Ranieri is a bell'. Hey, hey!"

Claudio Ranieri

Ian Baker: "What criticism are you talking about?"

Nigel Pearson: "Have you been on holiday for six months? Have you been away for six months?"

IB: "I am not quite sure what specific criticism you are referring to?

NP: "I think you must have been either head in the clouds or away on holiday or reporting on a different team because if you don't know the answer to that question, your question is absolutely unbelievable, the fact you do not understand where I am coming from. If you don't know the answer to that question then I think you are an ostrich. Your head must be in the sand. Is your head in the sand? Are you flexible enough to get your head in the sand? My suspicion would be no."

IB: "Probably not."

NP: "I can, you can't. You can't. Listen you have been here often enough and for you to ask that question, you are either being very, very silly or you are being absolutely stupid, one of the two because for you to ask that question, I am sorry son, you are daft."

IB: "There hasn't been much harsh criticism of the players."

NP: "You are wrong. No, you are wrong. You have been in here, I know you have so don't give that crap with me. I will smile at you because I can afford to smile at you. Now do you want to ask a different question or do you want to ask it differently. Come on, ask it. Ask it or are you not capable?"

IB: "I just don't know what you, erm…"

NP: "You don't know. What's erm?"

IB: "I don't know how you've taken that question."

NP: "Well you must be very stupid. I'm sorry."

Pearson's bizarre row with a journalist

Pat Murphy: "Why can't you be more specific about the criticisms of your players. In the media, we're a bit baffled by that because we think we've been very supportive of your players this season."

Nigel Pearson: "Do you? OK, that's your opinion."

PM: "I know but could you give us a specific example of disagreement."

NP: "No, I don't feel that I want to get into that sort of an argument with you."

PM: "But you're generalising about us."

NP: "You generalise about me, so there you go."

PM: "I'm giving you specific examples, I know how supporting the media have been."

NP: "Do you?"

PM: "Yeah, I can't accept this, at all, that we're after you."

NP: "I didn't say you were after me. I said there has been criticisms and I'll stick up for my players."

PM: "Many, many people have been saying that things have not gone your way."

NP: "I think you are looking through your side of the argument through rose-tinted spectacles."

PM: "Well it takes two to tango."

NP: "It does indeed."

PM: "You were the one who had a go at one of our reporters, in my opinion, unfairly."

NP: "There you are. I think we've come into some criticism, and so have I, when I think it's unfair."

PM: "Surely it comes with the territory."

NP: "Well there you go then, absolutely."

PM: "When did it dawn on you to apologise?"

NP: "I don't think that's something which I need to answer. I've apologised and I would, if it had been a more private thing, apologised one-to-one."

Pearson is challenged about his remarks

THE FUNNIEST LEICESTER QUOTES... EVER!

Reporter: "Steve Bruce cited Chelsea in terms of how the Leicester players behaved to try and get Alex Bruce sent off…"

Nigel Pearson: "Did they? Oh very nice."

Reporter: "Do you think that's a fair criticism?"

NP: "No."

Reporter: "What's your take on that situation?"

NP: "I've just said no."

Reporter: "But what's your take on a situation where all the players surround a referee?"

NP: "How many times have you seen us play this year?"

Reporter: "Three times."

NP: "Well there you are then. You're not in a position to judge my players on that."

Reporter: "I'm not judging anyone. I'm just

asking you…"

NP: "You've asked me and I've told you. No was the answer. I don't think it's a fair assessment. Full stop."

Reporter: "Do you consider that Leicester's season is waxing or waning?"

NP: "I don't have to use that sort of analogy. We are in the same position. We've got 10 games left, six games at home, and our home form has to be drastically improved for us to give ourselves the best chance. That's it. You got any more questions you want to ask? Obviously not. Yep good thank you. Waxing or waning, f*cking hell. My a*se. Pr*ck."

Press conference exchange following Leicester's 0-0 draw with Hull City

PLAYER POWER

"After games, we would have chicken burgers and potato wedges and he then changed them to sweet potatoes and pasta. I understand his point but the lads liked what we were used to, chicken and wedges."

Danny Simpson is upset Claudio Ranieri tinkered with players' dinner

"[Brian Clough] had a real go at the young [waiter]. It made me distinctly embarrassed and it looked, and sounded, dreadful. There was absolutely no need for that row."

Gary McAllister on his move to Forest breaking down

"He's really aggressive. You might walk into the physio room and you'll be getting headlocked by someone and it'll be him. Or when he goes to shake your hand in the morning, you'll hear your knuckles clicking. And then he doesn't let go because he enjoys inflicting pain on people. He genuinely does."

Ben Chilwell on Caglar Soyuncu

"I always feel quite lucky going into a game if Catherine has just shaved my head. Every time she did that at Oxford, I seemed to score a goal."

Matt Elliott on his wife helping his game

"Frank would often report to the ground at 2pm, then disappear for half an hour. More often than not he'd be signing autographs in the car park or grabbing the numbers of some admiring females!"

Alan Birchenall on Frank Worthington

"I always take my right boot off at half-time as the circulation around the big toe isn't too good. I like to give it a little wiggle."

Matt Elliott's interesting superstition

"He is like your favourite teacher at school."

Robert Huth on Claudio Ranieri

"I fill a small plastic water or Lucozade bottle to halfway and just sip the port while watching television. It tastes like Ribena to me, and it helps me switch off and get to sleep a bit easier the night before a game."

Jamie Vardy

Interviewer: "The size of your head – is it a family trait?"

Harry Maguire: "Yeah I blame my dad, ha."

Interviewer: "Any nicknames?"

Maguire: "Vards always calls me Slab Head."

Interviewer: "That's not very complimentary."

Maguire: "Not really. I've got a few for him but I'll keep them off camera!"

"In training, it was so easy for him that I was convinced that he intentionally gave the ball away sometimes just to enjoy winning it back again. Once he said to us that he was seriously considering running to the training centre each day."

Jamie Vardy on N'Golo Kante

"You don't live in a democracy when he is in charge – it's more of a Martocracy."

Kasey Keller on working under manager Martin O'Neill

"There's more meat on a toothpick."

Alan Birchenall on Robbie Savage

"I feel betrayed by Ranieri and let down by the club. I will not play for them again."

Leonardo Ulloa after his agent had said: "Ranieri is behaving like a selfish, egocentric egotist."

"He walked in and slammed the door behind him and started going, 'You, ya wee English sh*te, ye', and he's looking straight at me. He walked up to me – I was tiny in those days – and he picked me up by the scruff of the neck and pinned me against the dressing-room wall. I was trembling. I wouldn't have minded but we were two up at half-time and I'd scored them both!"

Gary Lineker on Jock Wallace

"Getting over Martin O'Neill is proving very difficult for me and I don't know how long it will take me to recover. I have to hide the fact that I miss Martin as much as I do."

Neil Lennon

"If I am so tough, why do my teammates call me Lily?"

Robbie Savage insists he's no hard man

"Hi, this is Jamie Vardy from Vardy News – what is the diameter of your head?"

Jamie Vardy gate-crashes one of Harry Maguire's England interviews

"It was a case of, 'Call me Jock' as he met my parents and made them a cup of tea and they thought he was lovely. Taking his advice, the following day I walked into Filbert Street, met him in the corridor and said, 'Morning, Jock'. He smacked me in the back of the head and told me never to call him by his first name again. It was a rude awakening, a harsh introduction. It took me a year to recover from the thump."

Gary Lineker on manager Jock Wallace

"We should call him Baloo from The Jungle Book because of his big bear's backside."

Kasey Keller on Matt Elliott

CAN YOU MANAGE?

"I'm fed up with my career going backwards because my team has been sold from underneath my nose. Before I die, I wanted to have the chance to spend some money. There was a bomb ticking and if it had gone off and somebody else had got the job I would always have felt the bridesmaid. The game, the business, stinks sometimes but I don't. I would have been a liar if I had stayed at Plymouth."

Ian Holloway gives an honest assessment on why he left Plymouth for Leicester

"When you win, you feel 25 years old. When you lose, you feel more like 105."

Gordon Lee after losing 5-2 to Swindon

"At Valencia, I won the Copa del Rey for the first time in 25 years. I can stop or shall I continue? Also in Greece I wanted to build something but it's difficult to build on the sand."

Claudio Ranieri reacts to criticism of his Foxes appointment

"Am I disappointed with the reaction? Yes. I understand but I will work hard to make changes. I respect everybody. But now my problem is not Lineker or Redknapp or Mark Bosnich. My focus is on Leicester."

Claudio Ranieri responds further to the critics

"I feel like I have been acting in Coronation Street all my life and now I am King Lear. I just felt I couldn't turn this down. I can't wait to get started. This is a whole new challenge which throws me into a whole new ball park."

Ian Holloway after taking the Leicester job

"I think everyone now rotates. The Tinkerman was one, now there are a lot of Tinkermen!"

Claudio Ranieri on his old nickname

"I've come from caviar to fish 'n' chips. At Spurs you can buy daft. At Leicester I have to buy sensibly."

David Pleat

"One day maybe, when I've gone or I am waving goodbye to this earth, but not now. In Italy we say if you get a monument it's because you're dead. So, just wait to make the monument."

Claudio Ranieri on calls to erect a statue in his honour

"I'd like to be remembered as a decent manager, but when you look up: 'Micky Adams Leicester City', what comes up? It's not saving a club from administration. It's not getting promotion. It's not playing in the Premier League. It's La Manga."

Micky Adams rues the team's trip to Spain which saw three of his players thrown in jail

"Statistically, I'm currently the worst Leicester manager in history and that doesn't sit well with me. On my gravestone it will say, 'Here lies Ollie – he tried'. I will never give up."

Ian Holloway always gives 110 per cent

"My youth coach told me he'd got these two great 15-year-olds. I told him I don't want to know, because by the time they're 18, I'll be dead."

Martin O'Neill

Reporter: [After winning the title] "What should your new nickname be?"

Claudio Ranieri: "The Thinkerman."

"Sir Claudio? Unbelievable! Has somebody called me? No, nobody, but I like it! Don't joke, please!"

Claudio Ranieri on calls for him to be knighted

"I look in the mirror and think, 'Cor dear, 'oo's that?' But I don't spend long looking. It's not a pretty sight."

Dave Bassett

"I was sitting there during the game thinking to myself: 'I can't believe this – I am manager of England'."

Peter Taylor as England caretaker manager against Italy

"Before I was the Tinkerman and now it's the same!"

Claudio Ranieri on criticism he's not rotating his players

"Ah, the image! I saw in the past a lot of images with different managers. They had a fantastic image, but now their teams play in the Championship."

Claude Puel defends his public persona

"It's scary. Frightening. How did this 'appen? I'm still a young kid. I'm just basically mad, really."

Dave Bassett on turning 60

"Managing a football club is like gardening. At Brentford I took a chainsaw to it. I don't know what I will be doing at Leicester yet."
Incoming boss Martin Allen

"I feel a bit like a pantomime villain sitting here."
Craig Shakespeare after Claudio Ranieri's sacking

"I waited so long but I am so happy. I don't know what will happen next season because this was a magic season. After the last match, let me go to the sea and recharge my batteries. And after that we will start."
Claudio Ranieri looks back on the title win

THE FUNNIEST LEICESTER QUOTES... EVER!

BOARDROOM BANTER

"There's no rift with him, we get on really well. I don't know where these stories come from, but if I thought about things like that I would end up sat in a room banging my head against a wall."

Martin Allen laughing off reports of a rift with his chairman Milan Mandaric

"Leicester City this evening announced that they had parted company with manager Martin Allen by mutual consent. Differences between both parties regarding the direction of the club have led to a breakdown in the relationship."

Just two days later, the club releases this statement

"We will move heaven and earth to keep Emile at Leicester."

Chairman Sir Rodney Walker – just a day before he sold the striker to Premier League rivals Liverpool

"Mr [Neil] Warnock is a talented manager but has never scaled any great heights for reasons he might wish to consider in a less self confident and brash frame of mind."

Chairman Jon Holmes makes his feelings clear on the outspoken Sheffield United manager

"I made a gentleman's agreement that would have allowed me to talk to Leeds, but obviously my chairman has Alzheimer's disease or something. I will never have dinner with him again."

Martin O'Neill on his decision to remain as Leicester manager

"We can't turn around now and say Paulo needs to go. Now is the time for us to show how strong we are together, how united we are behind our manager and give him a chance."

Chairman Milan Mandaric one day before sacking Paulo Sousa. Sven-Goran Eriksson was in place two days later

"One day before a game [owner] Vichai [Srivaddhanaprabha] came knocking on my door. His son was with him and five yellow-clad Buddhist monks. The monks wrote something on my desk and gave me a piece of paper to stick in my pocket. Vichai was convinced that we would win after that. But we didn't and I never saw those monks again."

Sven-Goran Eriksson

"He's a kitten after what I've had before."

Ian Holloway on his Foxes chairman Milan Mandaric

THE FUNNIEST LEICESTER QUOTES... EVER!

CALLING THE SHOTS

"I told him he was playing and he smiled. I told him he was marking Juninho and he went white."

Martin O'Neill to defender Pontus Kaamark before the game with Middlesbrough

"If he wants to come here, I will open the door and stand and wait for him in the door."

Sven-Goran Eriksson says the door is open for Owen Hargreaves to sign

"Gerry Taggart likes to think he came to Leicester under the Bosman ruling, but that's just another way of saying free transfer."

Martin O'Neill

"The players bought each other presents and there was a bit of mickey taking which was a bit pornographic."

Dave Bassett plays down a clash between Dennis Wise and Robbie Savage at the 2001 Christmas party. Wise reportedly presented Savage with the Secret Santa gift of a teddy bear in a Leicester shirt with a sex toy attached to it, with the message: "You're the only pr*ck in a Leicester shirt."

"I'll help you pick the team, boss. It will be just like our days at Wimbledon."

Savage's riposte to Wise, referring to his close relationship with Bassett from their Wimbledon days

"Mike is not just a 'yes' man. He is not just a Muppet that nods his head every day. He will have an opinion and I like that."

Martin Allen on Mike Stowell's appointment as goalkeeping coach

"Ian Marshall has been fantastic for us. When he's fit, he's superb. It's just that he's never fit."

Martin O'Neill

"Sometimes the French mentality is, today I play well, maybe I'll play well tomorrow."

Claudio Ranieri on Man United striker Anthony Martial

"My team is like the RAF – beep, beep, beep! I love it. When you want to build something, it's about the club. The head of the fish. That's the secret."

Claudio Ranieri compares Jamie Vardy, Marc Albrighton and Jeffrey Schlupp to the RAF after they are named among the fastest players in the Premier League

"I don't consider signing Stan [Collymore] a risk at all. He'll enhance the dressing-room spirit because he's a bright lad."

Martin O'Neill, a week before Collymore sprayed a Spanish hotel lobby with a fire extinguisher

"One evening, I'm having my dinner and I thought, 'Blimey, this is a bit salty'. But I didn't want to complain to the chef and I finished it off. 'Pelican Head' had put half a salt cellar in it. Years later, I always hold him responsible for my cardiac arrest. He's the one that nearly finished me off!"

Alan Birchenall on Robbie 'Pelican Head' Savage

"I have known people get over AIDS more quickly than Marshall has recovered from hamstring trouble."

Martin O'Neill on injury-prone striker Ian Marshall

"This player Kante, he was running so hard that I thought he must have a pack full of batteries hidden in his shorts. He never stopped running in training. I had to tell him, 'Hey, N'Golo, slow down. Slow down. Don't run after the ball every time, OK?' He says to me, 'Yes, boss. Yes. OK'. Ten seconds later, I look over and he's running again. I tell him, 'One day, I'm going to see you cross the ball, and then finish the cross with a header yourself'. He's unbelievable, but he is not the only key. There are too many keys to name in this incredible season."

Claudio Ranieri on his midfielder N'Golo Kante

"Gerry [Taggart] pal, what have I f*cking told you? How long have you been with me now? You can give the ball to Lenny [Neil Lennon]. You can give the ball to Muzzy [Izzet], but don't give it to f*cking [Robbie] Savage, you know he can't play football!'."

A Martin O'Neill half-time rant, as told by Gerry Taggart

"Wes Morgan is Baloo off the Jungle Book. He is a big gentle bear who looks after all the lads."

Claudio Ranieri on Wes Morgan

"This is not a footballer. This is a fantastic horse."

Claudio Ranieri on Jamie Vardy

"Thankfully he didn't go to Ibiza. I think he has made the right decision!"

Craig Shakespeare on Jamie Vardy looking to work as a club rep

"I keep telling the same joke over and over again about Kante: No matter who we're playing, we play three in midfield. We play Danny Drinkwater in the middle as a holding player and we play Kante either side!"

Foxes head of recruitment Steve Walsh

"Muzzy Izzet? I'm just in love with that young man."

Martin O'Neill

OFF THE PITCH

"George Best had a reputation with the ladies but I had more than my fair share. There's one story about how I managed to seduce a Swedish teenager and her mother. They were great days."

Frank Worthington

"At the end of the day I haven't killed anybody. A million players have done it and a million more will do it in future."

Stan Collymore after he let off a fire extinguisher in a hotel lobby on a club tour

"Chat sh*t get banged."

Jamie Vardy's now famous Facebook post

"You tell them Claudio even rotates the books!"

Claudio Ranieri after revealing to a reporter he is reading three books at the same time

"I ran out of petrol on the motorway. I phoned the police and they asked my name. I told them 'Dave Bassett'. This cop said, 'The Leicester manager?' I said 'yes' and he burst out laughing."

Dave Bassett

"Robert De Niro would be good. I've heard that's who they want to play me!"

Claudio Ranieri on his screen actor for a Hollywood movie

"Barry Hayles had a top on today that made him look like a traffic light. I don't know what the matter is with him."

Ian Holloway on his striker's fashion sense

Q: "At home, when was the last time you ironed a shirt?"

Mark Robins: "I pay my wife to do that."

"I am a calm person, even when I was young. I haven't been in a disco more than 10 times."

Claudio Ranieri is relaxed on the last day of the season

Q: "Who is your most dangerous opponent?"

Frank Worthington: "My ex-wife."

"They are in the public domain and people take advantage of them. Women are quite clever at knowing that men's hormones are very up and down. If you want to put it that way."

Dave Bassett on the pitfalls of being a footballer

Q: "What's your best advice to young players?"

Gerry Taggart: "Drink lots of beer and smoke loads of fags."

FIELD OF DREAMS

"My heart was just racing lying in bed. I didn't want the alarm to go off, I didn't want to wake up. I was petrified."

Ben Chilwell on the night before his first training session on loan at Huddersfield

"I used to do it all the time, it's just frustration. It is better to punch myself than somebody else isn't it! I've cut my lip quite a few times."

Jamie Vardy explains why he hits himself

"Now the sexy football show rolls into Leicester!!"

Robert Huth's bizarre tweet after completing his Leicester switch

"There's no pressure. Only weak people feel pressure."

Jermaine Beckford on his deadline day move from Everton

"When I was bored at home in the evening I'd pour myself a glass [of Skittle vodka], sit back and enjoy. The vodka was decent but it wasn't doing much for my dead leg, which didn't stop bleeding for ages. Dave Rennie, the physio, said he couldn't believe it wasn't improving. He'd seen a torn calf muscle heal quicker... He then explained the alcohol was damaging the healing process."

Jamie Vardy

"Yes! Champions League guaranteed! Better start practicing my Rabonas."

Robert Huth tweets his excitement

"I had no boots, so I did two training sessions and the first game with somebody else's. I don't even know whose they were."

Dennis Praet on arriving at Leicester

"The upshot of it is I faxed a transfer request to the club at the beginning of the week... but let me state that I don't want to leave Leicester."

Stan Collymore

"I always turn round and say, 'I don't think you should be singing that'. And the parents say, 'No it's all right, his cousin's called Charlie. He thinks he's turning up to your party with his cousin'."

Jamie Vardy on children singing the 'Jamie Vardy's having a party' song

"Loads of people are called Michael, but they're not associated with Michael Jackson, are they?"

Elvis Hammond is fed up with the "Elvis, give us a song" chant from opposition supporters

"I was watching the Blackburn game on TV on Sunday, when it flashed on the screen that George [Ndah] had scored in the first minute [for Wolves] at Birmingham. My first reaction was to ring him up. Then I remembered he was out there playing."

Ade Akinbiyi

"I enjoyed it so much, I'd go through everything again. The only thing I wish I'd done better was drive more carefully."

Gordon Banks on his professional career which was ended after a car crash in 1972 cost him the sight in his eye

"Thanks a lot Leicester!! It was unreal! A tip for the future... don't let centre halves take free-kicks."

Robert Huth's tweet on retiring

"Don't ask me about VAR. I don't know what it stands for."

Jamie Vardy after his England goal was cancelled out

"I don't know the words of the national anthem but I enjoy the Turkish culture and the food."

Muzzy Izzet on his Turkey call-up

"The last time I lifted a weight? Probably that can of Red Bull the other day."

Jamie Vardy

"Well then, let's hope Elvis is found alive."

Kasper Schmeichel after hearing the odds of Leicester winning the title were the same as someone seeing the legendary singer

"Going full John Terry today!! #fullkit #LCFC"

Robert Huth trolls John Terry after vowing to join Leicester's title celebrations wearing the full strip

"I am still in contract with Leicester so at the moment I am here and we will see. With me, especially, you never know what is happening. Every time I have to go, but I am still here. I don't really want to talk about whether I am going, or staying. We will see what will happen for me."

Riyad Mahrez is clear as mud

"People are always telling me there is a lot of skill in our side. You tell me where it is. There are one or two skilful players, and that's it. The rest are workers."

Frank Worthington has a not-so-subtle dig at his teammates

"I think it will be tougher against Tranmere. I expect to be more heavily marked. No disrespect to Argentina because they are obviously a great side."

Emile Heskey

"@EASPORTSFIFA taking the absolute p*ss with these stats!???"

Wes Morgan is not happy with his FIFA 20 rating, which included 29 for pace

"I could kiss him. I could really kiss his feet."

Christian Fuchs on Eden Hazard's goal for Chelsea against Spurs which sealed the title

"In France we didn't really [know Leicester] because they were in the Championship. I thought they were a rugby club."

Riyad Mahrez

"He put in his report that I've got hips like Barbara Cartland."

Tim Flowers on a specialist who said he may need a hip replacement in the future due to his arthritis

"An absolute full-kit w*nker!"

Jamie Vardy on meeting his lookalike wearing a Foxes strip

"Me and Johnno lay in the bath and we could hardly get out!"

Geoff Horsfield after he and Andy Johnson scored in a win over Coventry – despite having a combined age of 65

"After the Coca-Cola Cup final at Wembley I apologised to Juninho. I said, 'Sorry, but this is what I was told to do'. Morally, I don't enjoy man marking. I believe players should be free to express themselves. After all, this is show business."

Pontus Kaamark on keeping tabs on the tricky Brazilian

"I hope to score at least one goal and be better than Bosko Balaban!"

New signing Andrej Kramaric pokes fun at the fellow Croatian, who flopped at Villa

"Three Red Bulls, a double espresso and a cheese and ham omelette is what makes me run around like a nutjob on match day."

Jamie Vardy

"I was terrified on my first day. I had only just passed my driving test too, so getting to Leicester was a big nervous affair in itself!"

Alan Smith on joining Leicester

CALL THE MANAGER

John Motson: "2-2 with goals from Muzzy Izzet, but I've got to ask you about the boy [Robbie] Savage, what a game he had."

Martin O'Neill: "Yes, John, he only lacks one thing... ability!"

The manager takes a playful swipe at his hard-working midfielder

"If the referee stands by that decision, I have two wooden legs. I will be seeing this ref again in my dreams – and I won't be kissing him!"

Ian Holloway after skipper Patrick Kisnorbo was sent off against Sheffield United

"F*ck off and die."

Nigel Pearson abuses a Foxes fan during the final minutes of a defeat to Liverpool

"I replied to one idiot in the stands – if he doesn't like what he sees, then don't bother coming."

Pearson continues after the game

"He ought to be done away with. It's a shame he hasn't been topped before."

Dave Bassett on the theatrics of Tottenham's Mauricio Taricco

"We really go through it on the bench. When we were 2-1 up and Cambridge got a couple of late corners, the others were all laughing at me because I was curled up in a ball in the corner of the dug-out, saying, 'I hate this job'."

Brian Little

"I don't know how old I was at the start of the game, but I'm 93 now. It was a long, long time watching my team keep Wimbledon out. It was like 120 years in Alcatraz."

Martin O'Neill after his team's League Cup semi-final away-goals win

"He said something to me. I don't have to reveal anything, do I? I think I'm more than capable of looking after myself... I don't care what they think of me, I pay my tax bill... It's not helpful when the three fountains of knowledge on Match of the Day make a mountain out of a molehill."

Nigel Pearson on his bizarre touchline confrontation with Palace's James McArthur

"Ah Nigel Pearson is blaming MOTD for making a mountain out of a molehill. We'd best be careful in future, the fella can look after himself."

Match of the Day host Gary Lineker responds by tweet

"If that's a penalty, then I may as well say I'm Alec McJockstrap and wear a kilt."
Ian Holloway is angry with the officials

"At half-time I would have settled for us just getting a corner."
Martin O'Neill after his team come back from two down to force a cup replay with Chelsea

"Lilian Nalis's goal was terrific. I've been trying to explain to him what the English word 'fluke' means."
Micky Adams

"What is the point of talking to him, he's one of the most arrogant men I have met."

Nigel Pearson when asked if he would speak to the referee over some bad calls

"I can't comment on the sending-off [of Dion Dublin] without sounding like Mr Wenger. It was a hot day and the sun was in my eyes."

Micky Adams

"Even my missus could have seen that and she wasn't at the game."

Ian Holloway bemoans a penalty in a 2-0 loss to Coventry

"I'm going to go out and get lambasted on wine."

Martin O'Neill after winning the League Cup

"I'd have put my house, its contents, my entire wardrobe, my undergarments, my socks and my shoes on the fact that he would score. How he didn't, I have no idea."

Ian Holloway on a bad miss by Iain Hume

"I'm concentrating to be calm, but of course I'm very very happy inside. My blood is unbelievable."

Claudio Ranieri following Leicester's incredible title win

"I had a midfield so young they should have been in nappies. It was a debacle."

Ian Holloway after losing to Southampton

"I'll try not to apologise too much for the game but I'm glad I got in for free."

Micky Adams after a dull goalless draw with Southampton

"I'm just happy to get one over Mrs Doubtfire, but fair play to him – he's done wonders for Palace."

Ian Holloway on Neil Warnock

Printed in Great Britain
by Amazon